Walking through the Seasons

Observations and Reflections by

MARILYN WEBB NEAGLEY

Published by Wind Ridge Publishing, Inc.
Shelburne, Vermont 05482

Library of Congress Catalog Card Number:
ISBN: 978-0-615-21412-2

Designed by Suzanne Fay/Oh!Suzannah
Illustrated by Lynda Reeves McIntyre

PRINTED IN THE UNITED STATES OF AMERICA

Walking
through the
Seasons

Observations and Reflections
by

MARILYN WEBB NEAGLEY

Published by Wind Ridge Publishing, Inc.
Shelburne, Vermont

Spring

Summer

Fall

Winter

Author's Note

This little book of observations and reflections began with the influence of parents and other relatives. Having been raised on a farm, my mother simply liked everything best if it was "natural." My father was an outdoorsman who enjoyed the woods as much as his vegetable garden. When traveling, he often made a point of stopping at roadside springs for what became ritualistic sips of pure water. His mother and sisters were walkers who reveled in the pleasure of such basic beauty as a sunset.

An appreciation and understanding of nature was later deepened by photographer, Clyde H. Smith; philosopher, Justin Brande; ecologist, Dr. H.W. Vogelmann; *New York Times* columnist, Hal Borland and anthropologist, Mary Carse. A glimmer of Walking Through the Seasons appeared when, in the late 60s, I worked with public school children and teachers and, later, was in the position, as a former president of Shelburne Farms in Shelburne, Vermont, to envision and oversee the creation of an elementary school science curriculum, Project Seasons. In that same position, I also had the opportunity to initiate a public walking trail system.

Then and now, it is my hope that parents and educators will support the instinctive connection that children make with the natural world and that all who may need it will find joy, solace and sensibility in the changing seasons.

It is both pleasing and appropriate to have artist, professor and long time "walking buddy," Lynda Reeves McIntyre, as illustrator.

I am deeply grateful to naturalist writer, Gale Lawrence, for her inspiration, advice and encouragement and to the *Shelburne News* for first publishing these columns as Monthly Reflections and, now, for making this compilation possible.

. . . .

Two books by Donald W. Stokes, *A Guide to Nature in Winter* and *A Guide to Bird Behavior* (Volumes I and II) provided very helpful information. I highly recommend Gale Lawrence's *The Beginning Naturalist* as another important resource.

A childhood favorite, *An Introduction to Nature* by John Kieran and *A Modern Herbal* (in two volumes) by Mrs. M. Grieve, along with the *Peterson Guide Series* by Roger Tory Peterson and *Stalking the Wild Asparagus* by Euell Gibbons provided additional background, if only from memory.

For
Mark, Anna, Heidi, Sam, Jada and Ave

Spring

MARCH 18, 2003
Month of Water

March is, to me, the month of water, whether it appears as a stream raging down mountainsides, or as the subtler muddying of last year's soil and debris, pungently stale yet hopeful. It is not only in sight and smell that water makes itself known, but also in sound. Ice, dangling as slender pencils, chime in softening lakes and ponds. Frozen puddles attract children's feet for the simple fun of crunching. The thunderous movement of ice masses and the roaring boil of rivers announce a new beginning, year after year. Even the patient drip, drip, drip of sap tells us that change is underway and life is stirring again. We watch in awe as that sap transforms dull twigs into painterly yellows or reds.

When winter has been particularly long and difficult, I experience an extra thrill as the waters begin to move. Neighbors, barely seen in past weeks, may rush to watch as a nearby stream overflows its banks, changing the topography of all that was familiar. If lucky, such an event is witnessed when the moon is rosy and full, pulling in all its glory. When the thaw takes place and the waters move again, it is as though the earth itself, in a birth-like way, has broken open.

March, the mud season, is also the time of maple sugaring and tree pruning. It is a time that reminds me of childhood adventures in and around the Vermont village of Ascutney.

MARCH 5, 2004
Maple Syrup and Mud Season

Signaling the end of a long, still winter, murky days like these were thrilling. One could feel life stirring as the snow melted and earth softened. Hurrying home from school, my friends and I often walked a mile or so along a rutted dirt road to a farm on the outskirts of the village. There we were welcomed into a steamy sugarhouse and offered samplings of boiling maple sap. Farmers magically, as if by alchemy, turned the clear liquid into golden syrup. Then, without fail, a mother and her children would call to us as they brought scrumptious maple cake or fudge from the farmhouse. Their offering of spring sweetness, served over a patch of muddy ground, seemed to help us transition into spring.

Farther along that dirt road lived a boy named Herman McDerment. He once won a school contest, probably introduced by the county forester. To prevent further defoliation of trees by Eastern Tent Caterpillars, we school children were challenged to see who was observant enough to find and collect the most caterpillar egg masses. I felt very pleased to be a part of this community effort and proud to bring in six or eight branches, each with a small silvery band of 100 to 300 eggs. Herman, raised on a dairy farm, must have known that the eggs would be laid on cherry, apple, crabapple and possibly maple trees. I did not. He arrived at school on the final day of the contest with a hundred or so twigs. Needless to say, he won the prize… a flowering cactus that the teacher's son had recently brought from a trip to Arizona.

Although times have changed, these stories depict the pleasure derived from simply getting out and savoring the season at hand.

MARCH 12, 2005
The Sight and Sound of Crows

Although I spotted several Robins on March 5th, by the middle of this month it has not felt much like spring. Certainly the days are longer and the sun feels much warmer but repeated snowstorms have stalled the major thaw that we expect this time of year.

One seasonal sight and sound is that of the Crows. Most of them moved on to warmer places during the winter and have recently returned. Their many different "crackles and caws" are lively and wonderfully familiar. Crows gather in the afternoon to form communal roosts of 500 to 10,000 birds. Each morning they disperse to feed in small groups. Usually one sentinel bird calls out a warning to the rest of the flock if a predator appears.

As guardians of the woods and fields, Crows are wary and usually perch high in the trees making it difficult to approach them. It is, therefore, surprising that they can be good pets. I recall dining in a rather formal home several years ago when a child entered the room with a crow on his shoulder. The crow was quite well behaved. "Seated" high on the back of a chair, it occasionally took flight and silently swooped back and forth across the room.

To see these tall, black birds, glistening against the white of snow, is visually striking. In the months to come, as they forage in the greenness of a newly mown field, their sleek beauty will be unforgettable.

MARCH 19, 2006
Red-wings Return

The Red-winged Blackbirds have returned. Their thick, babbling song, so synonymous with spring, fills the air and is one of the most vital signs of this new season.

Easily identified, the male bears a bright red patch, bordered by a band of yellow, at the top of each wing. Most visible when in flight, the color appears in beautiful contrast with shiny black plumage.

I associate Red-winged Blackbirds with marshes, although they are also found in open areas where they feed on seeds and insects. Their cup-shaped nests, made by the female, are often placed near water within low reeds and rushes but may also be found on drier land in small trees or shrubs. Three or four whitish blue-green eggs with distinguishing dark scribbles are laid in each nest and incubated by the female.

Celebration of spring's annual arrival is greatly amplified by the conspicuous presence of *Red-wings.*

APRIL 15, 2003
Waiting for Spring

To experience spring one hundred times, is at least one hundred times too few.

As the sun, once again, begins to favor us, April announces a time of greening… and promise. Next to my home, small shoots and occasional blossoms respond to the warming light. Buds swell with fullness of anticipation while new blades emerge to overwhelm the bleached and discarded grasses of a year gone by. Wildlife has been noticeably active for some time but there is now a daring and visible work ethic in preparation for another growing season. The earliest flowers, affectionately called "pussy willows," have already been discovered and now other tree blossoms take on the happy hum of working bees. With amusing and blatant determination, birds haul cumbersome nesting materials in their perfect beaks, and then pause to sing.

Venturing farther from my back yard along formally and informally created footpaths, I explore the edge of a simmering pond as the purposeful activity of vivacious frogs warms the soul. Entering woodlands, a vein of limestone generously supports an exquisite treasury of native wildflowers. The wait for spring's unfolding has been somewhat longer this year but I am not disappointed. Rather, I am thoroughly heartened, once again.

APRIL 12, 2004
Shelburne Pond

At this time of year, one of my favorite places to visit is Shelburne Pond. As pussy willows begin to leaf out, frogs and salamanders become visibly active. The pond has changed little over the years and remains beautifully primitive.

This is also when the search for wild edibles begins. Leeks, milkweed shoots, yellow rocket and dandelion greens are among the tastiest. And I am certainly on the lookout for native flowers.

Perhaps spring has been slower to arrive this year. Recent walks have not yet revealed many wildflowers. Instead, patches of bright green moss in an otherwise khaki-colored woods, have caught my attention. These small, non-flowering plants form lush mats on trees, soil, rotting logs, and ledges. They serve as camouflage for tiny insects and provide fiber for nest-building birds.

Until this April, my own interest in mosses had been limited to building a terrarium or finding a soft seat. In the temporary absence of showy flower blossoms, a new appreciation has emerged.

APRIL 7, 2005
Progression of Spring

When the ice "goes out' and the water begins to warm, it is time to begin my annual trips to Shelburne Pond where I can observe the progression of spring. Along rich limestone shores wildflowers seem to come in waves, approximately two weeks apart. Spring Beauty and Hepatica, in frosty pastel colors, appear first. Later, muted green leaves unfold to display the strikingly white Bloodroot. Soon, while Dutchman's Breeches bloom, delicate white Saxifrage quietly emerges from rocky crevices. It is only then time for carpets of yellow Trout Lily, followed by the Common Blue Violet and an abundance of Trillium blossoms in shades of white, pink or maroon. Wild Ginger creeps across the ledges with its sturdy brown florets. At this point in the process, trees suddenly develop canopies of foliage, blocking the sun and changing the woodland habitat. April's magnificent display of early wildflowers comes to a close and I must wait a year to see them again. It is no wonder that state law protects these precious native plants.

While growth and change are taking place on land, the pond itself comes alive with frogs and toads, newts, birds and insects. It is difficult to believe that, only days before, all pond life had remained in frozen silence. At that time, tiny Pussy Willows had tiptoed in to announce the arrival of spring, but I barely noticed. The pleasant and unmistakable sound of Spring Peepers has finally summoned my full attention.

APRIL 10, 2006
The Magnificent Osprey

With warmer days, ponds, marshes and the lake beckon. Early in the month amphibious frogs, toads and salamanders found their way from land to water. Now, I have noticed that the magnificent Osprey has returned from coastal waterways. This bird of prey is sometimes called a "Fish Hawk" because it plunges feet-first from considerable heights to seize fish in its' iron-like talons. The fish, often remarkably large, is always carried away headfirst.

To spot an Osprey, I look near water at dead treetops or utility poles for giant nests made of sticks, seaweed, cornstalks and other odd material. Sometimes the Osprey is confused with an Eagle because of its wingspread of five feet or more and its white head. Yet, there is really no mistaking this bird, especially when observed in action, because it is the only large bird of prey in North America that is clear white underneath.

There are usually three eggs in a clutch. Sharp whistling *cheep, cheep* or *chewk, chewk* sounds of adult Ospreys are especially noticeable when, during breeding season, the air is alive with the clamor of their young. As fond parents, one usually stays with the nest while the other is fishing.

I am keeping my eyes open for the Osprey and the many other returning joys of April.

MAY 12, 2003
A Frenzy of New Life

One of the great pleasures of May is the sight of earth-brown fields created by the plows of farmers. Fertile fields, framed by the soft chartreuse of tender leaves or the mauve of lingering maple blossoms, reveal color patterns of unexpected beauty.

The season's rate of change is so remarkable that previously simple moments of observation have now become events. New grasses underfoot and overhead canopies of leafing trees take on an intensity of green. Earthworms, flooded from their homes by rain showers, remind us that, even through the deep freeze of winter, they never really went away. And we are glad for that. As the shad blooms white, meandering meadow streams glisten with marsh marigolds. A sweet violet, trout lily, trillium, and wild strawberry simultaneously appear, though not all in one place.

Twilight fills marshes with musical chatter. The crackling and exciting sound of red-winged blackbirds gives way to spring peepers, and others, who happily carry on well into the night. Then, in the earliest hours of daylight, songbirds disturb our sleep with exuberant pronouncements. As the days move toward mid-summer, groups of birds can be heard individually and sequentially, revealing who the early risers are. But, in May, there is such a frenzy of sound that concentration is required to distinguish one song, one bird, from the other. It is this frenzy that so astonishes and delights us, year after year.

MAY 5, 2004
In My Own Backyard

May was launched this year by warm south winds and a luscious preview of summer. The wind brought showers, so common and so necessary during the first week of this blossoming month. As tiny leaves unfold, the elegant Trillium and golden Trout Lily carpet woodland floors. Shad trees bloom and water-loving Marsh Marigolds, better known as Cowslips, accentuate green pastures. Even edible Morel mushrooms savor the rain and make an appearance. All of this within yards of my home!

It was my pleasure to recently spend the better part of a day with two "established" naturalists. We shared the pleasures found in walking the same path day after day. In a small, consistent area, changes that occur throughout the seasons can be dramatic. One of my companions recommended the observation of a grassy area as small as one square foot. In doing so, he said, "the diverse number of plants that can be counted is quite astonishing."

This conversation took me back to my twenties when, young and restless, I dreamed of far away places. One afternoon in his vast garden, an elderly Shelburnite and marvelous character, John Tracy, chided me, "You probably don't even know Limerick Road, and it's less than half a mile from your home." Well, generally speaking, Limerick Road is now the path that I walk, day after day.

MAY 5, 2005
Learning From Canada Geese

A few years ago, I had the pleasure of photographing the nesting season of Canada Geese. They had begun their process in April and, toward the middle of May, eggs began to hatch into fuzzy goslings. It was a thrill to observe their entire process and I continue to be inspired, year after year, by the sound of migratory "honking" and sight of air-borne flocks, often in a V-formation.

My daughter recently sent an article entitled, *Lessons from Geese,* by Angeles Arrien. The piece was intended to illustrate what wild geese can teach humans about leadership, collaboration, relationship and community. It's fun to discover the lessons taught by their natural behavior:

As each bird flaps its wings, it creates uplift for the next bird so that flying in a "V" pattern adds 71% greater flight range than when one bird flies alone. Whenever one falls out of line, it immediately feels drag and wants to quickly rejoin the uplifting formation, rather than going it alone. When the lead goose tires from maintaining the point of the "V," it rotates with another leader. Those at the rear honk encouragement to those at the front. Most amazingly, when a goose is ill or wounded, two others drop out of the pattern and follow their fellow member down to assist or provide protection. The caregivers remain with this member until it is well enough to fly or until it dies. Later, they catch up with their own flock or, if necessary, create a new formation.

What is most remarkable about Canada Geese is the commitment they make, not only to one another, but also to survival… to life itself.

MAY 7, 2006
Flowering Plants and Little Bees

When food was scarce during the earliest days of spring, "local" honeybees had discovered sweet sap oozing from a freshly cut birch tree. A couple of weeks later, they buzzed among maple blossoms in the treetops. Now in May, with so many flowers in bloom, bees can be seen everywhere.

Honeybees eat the nectar and pollen that are produced by flowers. The babies in each hive are fed pollen, or protein powder, by female worker bees to help them grow. Babies are born primarily in the spring, when flowers are most abundant. Sweet watery nectar is used by worker bees to make honey. Within their hives, bees store honey in hexagonal wax cells to be used as food in the winter. When a good supply of nectar and pollen have been located, a bee marks the spot with a scent, or pheromone, then returns to the hive and dances. The dance pattern tells the other bees in which direction and at what distance the food source can be found.

Because a flowering plant needs pollen from another plant to make seeds and reproduce, bees play an important role in helping with this process. Colorful petals, sweet nectar and fragrances entice the worker bees to land on blossoms. There they collect nectar and pollen. The yellow pollen dust attaches to them and, when it is deposited at the next flower, pollination occurs! Bats, butterflies, birds and the wind are also pollinators.

Flowering plants are an essential source of food and fiber including fruits, vegetables and grains, milk, blue jeans and lumber. Where would we be without flowers, little bees and the other pollinators?

Summer

JUNE 10, 2003
Arrival of Summer

Here in the Northern Hemisphere, the solstice occurs on approximately June 21st, marking the longest day of the year and the beginning of summer. Surrounded by growth and abundance, we fully embrace summer again. Wild strawberries are forming from what had been a simple spring blossom. The tiny seeds of each berry are embedded in a surface of sweet fruit, enticing a hungry bird or groundhog to help with transplanting. Anticipating future generations, determined turtles drag themselves to higher ground, in search of the perfect place to lay their precious eggs. Snapping turtles, in particular, with their ancient appearance, remind us of the vast time that has preceded us. The gnarly sumac's cones are graying and falling away, making room for this year's seed clusters of plush crimson. Spittlebugs appear on plant stems, cleverly concealed in frothy hide-a-ways, also working their way through a life cycle.

Wild edibles have been available for two or three months now but, in June, the foods that appear are easier to identify and satisfying to collect and prepare. It's an adventure to forage for cattail pollen. The yellow "flour," when sifted and blended with an all-purpose version, produces delicious pancakes. Buds of the day lily are tasty as dried or fresh additions to soup. Its lovely orange blossoms, open only one day, can be dipped in batter and fried.

As the wild plants and our gardens grow, there is a sense of satisfaction in knowing that, in June, summer is just beginning.

JUNE 9, 2004
The Plant World

June is a time of sparkling growth and abundance. While on a recent walk, I was struck by, not only the intensity of green, but also the multitude and variety of plants, each with a story of its own. One that continued to catch my eye along the path was Common Plantain. Identifiable as a broad-leaved "weed" with several densely flowered spikes, Plantain can be found along roadsides and in meadowlands. Thriving in soils we have disturbed, it tells scientists when and where humans have appeared. An herbalist would add that, among other curative properties, the bruised leaf of Plantain soothes insect bites.

As a young adult, my own awareness of the plant world was limited to my parents' vegetable garden, familiar plants such as clovers and daisies, and a few "odd" wild plants such as Skunk Cabbage and Jack-in-the-Pulpit. Then, through the informal teachings of a local herbalist and a university botanist, my eyes were opened. Even the tiniest plant, struggling to emerge from a crack in pavement, is now an attention-getter.

In contemplating plants we realize that they influence our lives in so very many ways. Whether experiencing spaghetti, a peanut butter and jelly sandwich, perfume, medicine or denim jeans, we have the plant world to thank.

JUNE 13, 2005
McCabe Brook Beavers

McCabe Brook, a very narrow stream located behind my home, has recently swelled into a rather impressive pond, thanks to the clever work of beavers. It has truly amazed me to see the precision with which they have engineered the construction of a dam, perfectly estimating the water level. Much like the tradition of a community barn raising, beavers from other families may join in the building of a dam. Using their front teeth and paws, a base or "foundation" is made with mud and stones. Brush and log poles are added. By placing the poles' more slender tips in the direction that the water flows, the dam is reinforced. Additional mud and stones, along with wet plants, are then used to plaster the poles. The beavers' territory is marked with *castors* or small piles of mud containing their scent.

There are two or more underwater entrances leading to an above water chamber or lodge. During the winter, a lodge may house several beavers. A Canadian study found that the lodge could maintain a temperature of 34 degrees F during winter air temperatures of –30 degrees F.

The broad, flat and rugged tail of a beaver comes in handy as a paddle or rudder but is most recognized by humans when heard as a loud slap on the water's surface, warning other beavers of danger.

A few evenings ago, I visited the new pond to catch a glimpse of its builders. A startling SMACK, which I chose to take as a greeting rather than a warning, was the only signal as to their whereabouts. Two heads eventually surfaced in the aquatic darkness then disappeared into a mysterious, and busy, underworld.

JUNE 19, 2006
Relentless Rain

On a recent morning I was awakened very early by a symphony of birdcalls. It struck me that the sound was more similar to that of early spring than of mid-June. I wondered how the birds had endured the relentless rain of recent weeks and whether it could be that their nesting season had been postponed. Interestingly, on that same morning the local daily newspaper published an article explaining that birds do suffer during such weather. Their nests, sometimes washed away, must be reconstructed. This later "re-nesting" season then causes a shorter maturation period, making the fall migration more challenging for young birds.

When the long period of gray, rainy days subsided, I was startled, yet reassured, to see that summer had been advancing as it always has. Snapping turtles were once again laying eggs in the back yard, spittlebugs had formed their bubbly homes and magical fireflies brightened the night sky. Life does indeed go on.

JULY 5, 2003
Month of Grasses

July is the month of grasses. From a distance, fields languorously sway in summer breezes or are sculpted by farmers into neat rows and geometric shapes. Roadsides billow in abundance with border grasses. Some are refined and delicate while others are tall and rugged. Pausing to look more closely at the familiar hay grasses, Timothy or Brome, I see exquisite purples and yellows suspended in the flower clusters. Corn, oats, rye, barley and wheat move toward maturity, forming indelible impressions on minds and landscapes as they make their way to our kitchens, at least figuratively.

With the rising heat of midsummer, the air and my own skin are sometimes indistinguishable. A rich and luxurious atmosphere is marked by the perfumes of newly mown hay, milkweed blossoms, and sweet white clover.

The work of gathering and harvesting in support of baby birds, bee colonies, wildlife, farm livestock and humans has intensified and will madly continue into the fall.

But this season is also a time for play. Non-native wildflowers, Daisies and Black-eyed Susans, transported here by early settlers, punctuate the grasses, reminding me of childhood and the whimsical, carefree days of summer.

JULY 12, 2004
Roadside Flowers

July roadsides are spectacular. I recently had an opportunity to drive in northern Vermont where the more rural highways are less manicured. Sandy shoulders and minimal mowing provide a perfect habitat to showcase "roadside wildflowers." Daisies and Black-eyed Susans appear everywhere. Eye-catching and sweetly scented borders seem to have been created by a professional landscaper. Tall, billowing stands of Sweet White Clover provide a backdrop for blue Chicory and, of course, the stocky Milkweed. In the foreground, perfectly edged, are delicate grasses amidst mounds of Trefoil and Rabbit-foot Clover. Most of these plants, and others, can also be found in more urban areas but may not be as beautifully presented as they are in the countryside, especially along the roads. Traveling with windows open, a warm breeze stirs the senses. To catch passing glimpses of luxuriant floral displays, and inhale their perfume, is to experience the richness, the essence, of summer.

JULY 5, 2005
Bird Song

For some time now, I have been awaking to the sound of birds. Each song seems to have higher volume and greater intricacy than the next. It is difficult to identify who the individual composer might be because all of the works have been layered. I think, in the wee hours of the morning, how barren life would be without the flight and melody of these feathered friends.

Yesterday, from the top of a nearby tree, a Robin proudly sang its heart out. Moments later, the whir of tiny wings caught my attention as a brilliantly painted Hummingbird hovered over the sweetness of honeysuckle. In the next moment, a female Cardinal, elegantly muted in color, strutted across the lawn, pecking here and there for food.

As the nesting period draws to a close, the musical sounds will diminish and it will be easy to forget them until next year. I can now see why some individuals have not taken them for granted and have made the study of birds a life-long occupation.

JULY 20, 2006
Newly Mown Hay

While walking along a dirt road very early this morning, I was reminded of the glory of summer. Have the Daylilies ever been as profuse as they are this year? Perhaps it is because of the rainy weather we had early on. In contrast to orange lilies, sky-blue Chicory has staked its claim on the landscape along with towering Mullein and bobbing Queen Anne's Lace.

And the grasses are so varied and lush. It is no wonder that one of mid-summer's most breath-taking sights is of hay, laid out in neat rows, following the earth's natural contours. Patterned fields and bordering trees rise to meet the rolling summer sky.

Several years ago I was taught that the wonderful scent of newly mown hay identifies a naturally occurring compound known as coumarin. It's found in such plants as lavender, sweet clover grass and licorice but also in food plants such as strawberries, apricots, cherries, and cinnamon.

Medically, coumarin has been shown to have anti- coagulant, anti-fungicidal and anti-tumor benefits and, because of its blood-thinning properties, it has also been used to poison rodents. First identified in the 1820's and synthesized in 1868, coumarin was evidently used by the Confederates to taint tobacco as way of getting revenge after losing the Civil War.

This morning's walk was an enjoyable exploration of summer but also of science and art. Good for the body, mind and soul.

AUGUST 11, 2003
Metamorphosis

Blankets of mist, layered between the warm earth and cooler night air, transform all that had been familiar. The rising sun gently unveils dew-covered meadows. Spiders have lavishly spun countless webs across the blades of grass. Summer is waning. Plants are not as lush and yet there is explosive ripening everywhere.

As summer progresses, the subtle beauty of Chicory or Queen Anne's Lace is replaced by striking masses of Goldenrod. I notice that the Goldenrod stems have sometimes swollen into spherical insect galls, creating simple habitats. It's amazing to discover ants productively "herding" aphids onto the same stems, just as we humans herd cows for our milk supply.

While feeding on milkweed leaves, a Monarch larva is easily collected and observed as it eventually metamorphoses into an elegant chrysalis of pale green and gold. Remarkably, as the small pouch darkens to blue and transparency, a magnificent butterfly soon emerges and takes flight.

Although there may be moments of remorse as the days shorten and shadows lengthen, August represents fulfillment and, in some ways, provides meaning for all of the other months.

AUGUST 7, 2004
Celebrating the Harvest

August begins with spectacular meteor showers and the glow of Goldenrod. Yet as the month progresses, summer begins to fade. The floating heads of Queen Anne's Lace look tattered and frayed. As the days go by, Ironweed, Boneset, and Asters, all the last flowers to bloom, make their appearance.

In the afternoons, crickets drowsily chirp and evenings are filled with the clamor of katydids. They have only a few more weeks. Most familiar bird sounds will soon disappear except for a few...the soft babble of the chickadee, the crackling call of the jay, and the taunting caw of the crow.

It isn't truly related to the calendar. Summer ends when ripeness begins, when the purpose of the season has passed. Last evening, dear friends prepared a meal for my husband and me. In celebration of August, they had gathered chanterelles in the woods and, combined with their own potatoes and leeks, prepared a creamy soup of earth flavors. Our main course was chicken served with string beans and robust beets, also from the garden. What a gift it was to be nourished by such bountiful food...a re-connection to the soil and to this remarkable time of year.

AUGUST 15, 2005
Common Milkweed

One of my favorite summer plants is the Common
Milkweed, easily found in open meadows and along
roadsides. It has many interesting phases, some of which are
considered edible to those who enjoy foraging for wild foods.
Although I won't pretend that they are delicious, tender stalks
found in early spring can be eaten as "pseudo-asparagus,"
if the water in which they are boiled is changed two or three
times. The same is true for the bud or "pseudo-broccoli" stage
found in late spring.

In summer, its dusty blossom, aromatic with an abundance
of nectar, attracts insects, especially honeybees. To guarantee
pollination, tiny slits in the florets trap its visitors. As they try
to free themselves, miniscule sacks of pollen, attached by a
thread, are caught on their legs and carried away. With close
observation we will see that some insects do not get away
while others attempt to fly with the burdensome weight of
tiny "saddlebags filled with gold."

In August, the Monarch butterfly, in its larval state, will
munch on milkweed leaves. Milkweeds contain glycosides
that can be poisonous to animals. The insects that do feed on
these plants develop immunity to the chemicals and, in many
cases, also become protectively poisonous or unsavory to their
predators.

And later still, when seedpods have matured, children
will take pleasure in the flight of feathery parachutes.

Finally, weathered stalks that are still standing in the
spring are useful to some birds, particularly orioles, which
strip them for nest building.

And so it goes, year after year.

AUGUST 15, 2006
Vocal Coyotes

Coyotes are generally heard at night or in the early morning but I have recently experienced them in the middle of the day, barking defensively, apparently in response to sirens or loud planes.

The Native American name for the coyote is "Little Wolf" as it is one of eight species of canines that includes the wolf and domestic dog. Found throughout North America, they are successful hunters, generally living on a diet of mice, rabbits, squirrels, other small rodents, insects, reptiles, wild fruits and berries. Coyotes are helpful in controlling the rodent population and generally stay to themselves but, on occasion, can be aggressive toward humans and have been known to eat small domesticated animals such as dogs and foals.

The coyote is one of the few wild animals that is commonly heard. Its vocalizations range from howling and yelping to barking and huffing, depending upon the circumstance. The well-known howl is intended to define territory but can also be a way of telling females they may approach while competing males may not. Their name, Canis latrans, means "barking dog" and refers to the sound made when protecting the den or making a kill. Usually the pups yelp in play and the barely audible huffing sound of the adults is used to herd the pups. When grouped together, coyotes may work themselves into a lather of yelps and howls and abruptly stop, altogether, at once.

Listening for the haunting calls of the coyotes creates a momentary link to their wild and mysterious world.

Fall

SEPTEMBER 7, 2003
Harvest Moon

It seems that all of life is in motion now, energized by crisper, cooler air and the anticipation of winter. Since the Harvest Moon is the full moon closest to the autumnal equinox, it will appear this year in September. As the Harvest Moon approaches, chipmunks and squirrels busily gather acorns. Humans stack wood and harvest foods from the garden or orchard. Monarch butterflies miraculously emerge to create visually striking images amidst deeply purple New England Asters. The Monarchs, along with migrating birds, prepare for long journeys to warmer places. Change becomes more dramatic when the first hard frost hits the valley. Colorful flowers and grasses fade while trees and shrubs may, for a brief time, take on brilliant color.

A simple walk reveals the season's activity. It is thrilling to discover a cormorant, heron, hawk and turtle in the area of one small pond.

In this transitional time, I savor the warmth of clear, sunny days and yet seek a glowing hearth on cool, starry nights. It is the sharply contrasting quality of September days that makes the onset of autumn so thoroughly enjoyable.

SEPTEMBER 5, 2004
Scattering Seeds

Yesterday, while walking on beautiful Shelburne Farms, I paused to engage in a little child's play. Impatiens was in abundance. Tall, translucent stems and red-spattered-orange blossoms make the plant easily identifiable. I found it amusing to pop the swollen seed pods that had formed over the summer. With the slightest pressure, the full pouches burst open; thus the plant's common name, "Touch-Me-Not." I tried to observe the explosion in slow motion, to count the number of seeds and see how they are actually propelled. Remarkably, four strands of the pod had peeled back rapidly enough to turn it inside out, forcing the tiny seeds to become airborne.

Seeds must be able to travel away from the parent plant in order to find the correct soil, light, moisture and nutrients in which to grow. In any given place there may be thousands of seeds waiting for conditions that will allow them to flourish. Downy wings of thistle, cattail or milkweed offer flight or birds and animals may transport and deposit ingested seeds. Clever hitchhikers such as burdock have Velcro-like designs for clinging to human clothing or animal fur. Seed dispersal and future growth are the ultimate goals of plants, guaranteeing that life goes on.

SEPTEMBER 12, 2005
Staghorn Sumac

So much has to occur in the few days between the maturation of summer and a killing frost. As time approaches the autumnal equinox, we are happily experiencing the fruit of Mother Nature's labor. Gardens, vines and orchards overflow while the eggs of snapping turtles hatch. The earth's fragrance is changing dramatically. Only two months ago the sweet smell of clover and milkweed filled the air. Now there is a rich aroma of nuts and spices. While changing locations from pond to field or forest, it is fun to guess how the various *perfumes* are made.

The Staghorn Sumac is a shrub or small tree that I particularly enjoy at this time of year. Often ignored, it is found in wastelands and thickets. Its branches resemble velvety deer antlers. Birds and wildlife feed on sumac's red, long-haired fruits and humans can boil and strain the fruits to make a "lemonade" of sorts. It is said that the leaves, which have the appearance of a tropical plant, can be boiled with the fruit to make a black ink. Sumac usually grows in clusters creating visually beautiful forms on the landscape and, as September progresses, the warm, rosy softness of its crimson hues will brighten your day.

SEPTEMBER 16, 2006
Goldenrod

While taking a brief walk near home, impressionistic splashes of orange drew my eyes to a field of Red Clover, our state flower. Taking a closer look, I saw that dozens of Monarch butterflies were drifting from one blossom to another, sipping sweet nectar. They were preparing to join the nearly billion other monarchs in migratory flight to the Mexican mountains.

Continuing on, my path became tunnel-like as it meandered through a tall stand of Goldenrod, or *Solidago juncea*. Here, it was the loud hum of honeybees and bumblebees that caught my attention. They were busily feeding on the attractive sprays of countless tiny "ray" and "disc" flowers, best seen with a hand lens. The group name, Solidago, stems from a Latin word that means "solidify" or make whole, referring to the healing powers that ancient physicians believed the plants possessed. More recently, people have considered Goldenrod to be the cause of "hay fever" but it is now known that this plant is no guiltier than other pollen producing plants and that the true culprit is, in most cases, Great Ragweed.

In late summer and early fall, bright and glorious Goldenrod heralds the colorful autumn beauty that is soon to follow.

OCTOBER 13, 2003
Month of Leaves

October is the month of leaves. Even without wind, autumnal leaves fall slowly, gently to the ground. Along with lifeless pine needles, they blanket our pathways and freshen the air. People come from miles away to enjoy with us the last display of brilliant color before the onset of winter. Decaying plants mix with moist soil to make a simple compost stew and fill the atmosphere with the clean aroma of earth and roots. Sharply clear skies come alive with the thrilling sight and sound of migrating geese. We hear their exclamatory chatter and, if attentive, the more subtle whisper of feathered wings in motion. The joy of piled leaves, the discovery of a Wooly Bear, or the flight of a downy milkweed seed gladdens the heart.

Fencerows call for our attention with their deep wine-like hues. They reveal their great value while defining elegant field patterns. Upon examination, we can now see the wealth that has been concealed in recent months. Wild grapes, berries, nuts and hollow trees provide an essential haven for wildlife. "Living on the edges," with the protection and sustenance of their fencerows, wildlife can more safely venture into open spaces.

The harvest is concluding and we will soon be settling in. Yet, during these recent glorious days of October, punctuated by golden leaves and silvery moon, we have paused to acknowledge and celebrate our great bounty.

OCTOBER 7, 2004
Dead Creek

A couple of days ago, I explored the Dead Creek in Addison, VT. It was one of those perfect October days. Heading north, I maneuvered my kayak over small waves in search of migrant ducks and geese. Torn and discolored, bygone lily pads tossed in the breeze. Purple clusters of arrowroot leaves, too, were weathered. In striking contrast to the vibrant foliage of trees and shrubs found elsewhere, marsh reeds, altered by frost, had taken on an elegant, antique finish with old tones of gold and teal. The water's smooth, onyx surface was disrupted by masses of jade-green duckweed. Moisture and decay had created a comforting atmosphere of fresh mustiness.

Turning off the main waterway, I entered a narrow channel. A dragonfly passed by. There, inevitably, stood a Great Blue Heron. Seemingly prehistoric, with overly long neck, legs and wings, it lifted out of the water and disappeared. For the next hour the heron and I played hide-and-seek. Each time I turned a new corner, it reappeared only to promptly disappear again.

Eventually it was time to head for home. Paddling south with the sun on my face and the wind at my back, I remarked, inwardly, at the simple pleasures of life.

OCTOBER 7, 2005
LaPlatte River

October began with summery temperatures. Yet, as cooler conditions will inevitably occur, we can look forward to an encore of beauty before the trees, baring and bracing for winter, lose their colorful leaves.

On one recent morning I was skimming across Shelburne Bay in my kayak. The air stirred only where warm morning sun touched the water's cooler surface. The sky and lake merged in the palest of blue. A burnished green ribbon of reeds bordered the bay, providing shelter for contented ducks. There was a deep sense of peacefulness.

After a while, I turned and paddled into the La Platte River. A whitish object became visible in a distant tree. Upon closer inspection I could see that a large Black-Crowned Night Heron perched overhead. Sitting sideways, its red-orange eye focused directly on my eyes and seemed to challenge me with, "Are you going to leave, or am I?" I respectfully left, thrilled at heaving seen such a striking bird.

Once again, setting aside the time to enjoy the natural world was profoundly rewarding.

OCTOBER 6, 2006
Bats

With Halloween just around the corner, this is a good time to reflect on bats. These small mammals roost upside down, in trees, caves, and structures. They are not blind but have better vision at night than in daylight. Their high-pitched sounds bounce off objects, returning to the bats as echoes, helping to locate insects and other objects.

In recent weeks bats had been flying dangerously close, criss-crossing tree-lined walkways. They were, in fact, so close that I made loud sounds to aid their system of eco-location in hopes that they would easily detect and avoid me. Now, while walking at dusk in cooler temperatures, I notice that they are no longer swooping overhead. With the scarcity of insects and pollen bearing plants, they are either hibernating or have migrated, or a combination of both.

It is unfortunate that, because of negative myths about bats, we sometimes forget their valuable roles in controlling insects, pollinating plants, and, of course, setting the stage for Halloween.

NOVEMBER 9, 2003
Dark Days and Stellar Nights

Aesthetically speaking, November is restrained and subtle, handsome and refined. Now that most of the leaves have fallen, the lines of trees are visible again. On a damp or rainy day, the trees appear to us as ink-black etchings made more beautiful by spectacular points of color. It may be the deep red dots of frost-bitten fruit scattered among or below the gnarly crown of an apple tree or russet leaves delicately attached to a Beech tree. Landscapes, with golden or nut brown fields surrounded by the spatter-paint of rust, ochre, burgundy and dark evergreen, resemble an elegant fabric of woolen tweed. On a dark, cold day, our favorite pathway may feel sunny in the golden glow of fallen maple leaves. Revealed now are contours of rolling hills and expansive views of the horizon.

November days can often be heavily gray and moody, making the horizon less visible. Watch for those days. That is when unexpected breaks in thick, low-lying clouds give way to patches of deep blue. Theatrical rays of sun may suddenly appear to spotlight a particular hillside or some other forgotten view and it takes our breath away to be reminded, awakened. At night, the thinning of tree canopies and cold, clear air make the sky more visible and provide an opportunity for stargazing. Of the billions of stars amidst hundreds of thousands of galaxies, we humans can see with the naked eye only 2,000, or so, from any one point on earth. Pondering the vastness of the universe provides a useful perspective on life.

Magnificently dark November days and stellar nights give us pause for such reflection.

NOVEMBER 4, 2004
Natural Compost

November is my favorite month. Muted by shorter, darker days and only a skeletal landscape, it is a time of vulnerability and subtle beauty. The earth, through its natural process of composting, neatly cleans away the summer residue before winter's period of rest.

Now, all that remains of a robust growing season are remnants...leftover pumpkins and apples, whispering ghost-like corn stalks, bittersweet splashes of color amidst bony branches. Leaves, nuts and berries blanket the ground, slowly decomposing, sometimes re-seeding. Where has all the life gone? How do the frost, wind, rain and sun make it all so tidy? How can it be that, after such productivity, we do not walk in unhealthy decay or among rotting animal carcasses?

Walt Whitman, in *This Compost,* posed such questions: "O how can it be that the ground itself does not sicken? How can you be alive you growths of spring? How can you furnish health you blood of herbs, roots, orchards, grain? Are they not continually putting distemper'd corpses within you? Is not every continent worked over and over with sour dead?"... He then advised us to "Behold this compost! Behold it well!" There is no better time to heed his advice, to observe in awe, than during the days of November.

NOVEMBER 9, 2005
Dramatic Sky

Now that trees are essentially bare, the November sky, in all its glory, is revealed again. Although the days are shorter and darker, sunsets shine with silver or red. Heavy, ink-colored clouds give way to brilliant rays of light. The less-than-full moon glows within a prismatic ring and showcases a single star.

Sweet fragrances of summer are a distant memory. Cooler temperatures have fermented lingering fruit. Nuts and leaves have dropped to the ground. A smoldering mixture of soil and decay fill the air with the exhilarating smell of earth and spice.

Soon, we will experience new fallen snow. The atmosphere will be clean and clear. What little color remains, thanks to the oaks and beeches, will be dramatized by whiteness. The hardy greens of mosses, ferns and conifers will offset the graying landscape.

Perhaps it is the dramatic contrasts of November that stirs the soul and makes a person glad to be alive.

NOVEMBER 12, 2006
Sensing Autumn

On a particularly sunny and warm day this November, I paused to sit at the edge of a pond to, not only see the beauty, but also to listen for the sounds of late autumn. With eyes briefly closed, I heard the fine rustle of dried grass and leaves. A few crackling beech and oak leaves remained but most deciduous trees were now too bare to snuff out the soft whisper of gentle breezes among the pines.

The sounds turned my attention to the many dried weeds around me. Though they may appear to be lifeless in November, many continue to thrive through their seeds and underground roots. It's interesting to observe the ways that weeds disperse their seeds, adapt to their environments, are useful to animals, or are simply beautiful in color and form.

Passing through the landscape, I looked for thorn or burr-bearing thistles and burdock or weeds with seedpods such as mustard and noticed the tall, familiar cattails or mullein and the, now, smoky gray masses of Goldenrod. Black-eyed Susans and Milkweed punctuated what would otherwise be dull waysides. The list goes on and on, even for those who live in urban areas because, happily, weeds prefer land affected by humans.

Winter

DECEMBER 7, 2003
Winter Solstice Approaches

As winter solstice approaches, the natural world is changing. It's somewhat simpler now. My attention turns from the dazzle of autumn colors to nearly black and white. No longer awed by a red or yellow leaf, I am now mesmerized by the intricacy of frost patterns and crystalline snowflakes. Appearing as thousands of tiny stars, frozen water droplets, illuminated by the moon, adorn every plant in sight.

With fallen snow, tracks reveal the activity of wildlife. I try to guess what saga might have taken place, where each critter lives, and what it likes to eat. Now, the nests of birds and squirrels are exposed, revealing what had before been kept a secret. Nearly all of the buds have formed in preparation for next spring. It is fun to identify the names of trees and shrubs by looking at their twigs.

In this simpler winter setting, evergreens take on new meaning. While deciduous trees cast off their more dramatic beauty to take a rest, the enduring evergreens patiently go on. I stop and listen to the whisper of a pine as a gentle winter wind passes through. Or, gather greens for the freshness of their scent, bringing winter closer to home.

With increased cold and decreased light I enjoy the stark beauty of winter but seek the warmth and cheer of candlelight, a fireplace, holiday festivity…time for personal reflection or sharing with one another.

DECEMBER 10, 2004
Snowflakes

Snowflakes differ in size and shape. No two are alike. As masses of tiny ice crystals grow from water vapor in the clouds, all flakes grow in either plate-like or columnar patterns and all have six sides. Snow varies depending upon temperature, altitude and moisture. In some parts of the world, there are many names to describe the different types of snow.

Snow is sometimes scorned as burdensome or even dangerous but many enjoy its recreational value. It is also appreciated as an important source of water, an insulator and a protector of plants and animals.

Two past Vermont residents have contributed greatly to my own enjoyment of snow. Snowflake Bentley, through photography, opened my eyes to the marvelous crystals, each with its own geometric design. His work reminds me to take the time to catch a falling snowflake and appreciate its beauty and uniqueness. Robert Frost, through poetry, described the woods on a snowy evening. His words, "The woods are lovely, dark and deep," conjure an image of silent beauty.

In this month of the winter solstice, I look forward to watching the first snowfall drape the land like a great white blanket. All will glisten with bluish light. The air will smell so fresh and clean. And the world will seem to stand still.

DECEMBER 11, 2005
Chickadees and Others

A friend and I recently embarked on a walk in the Adirondacks. We were startled by the sudden commotion of a jubilant flock of Chickadees. The trail's gatekeeper had left a pile of birdseed on the front porch of his modest cabin. The fluttering commotion of these small birds made me smile. I recalled nature writer, Hal Borland, and his apt description of them... "jaunty little friends, dressed in tuxedos."

This afternoon, a rather stark December day, my walk was again brightened by the "tseet-tseet" and the "dee-dee-dee-dee" of the Chickadees who called from various trees and shrubs. In the distance a crow cawed and a hawk swooped over snow-dusted fields. Everything seemed so still, except for the birds. Their presence is now less obvious than during the frenzy of spring but provides the same sense of awe, and comfort.

Interestingly, as I last week ascended the granite steps of an urban art museum, a pigeon landed next to my shoe. Its iridescent feathers caught my eye and, in a whisper, I tried to befriend it, as one might do with a dog or cat. "Stay near." The creature was somehow more familiar than the throngs of people pushing past me. I wanted it to linger.

Pablo Neruda, in *Birdwatching Ode,* having declared his love of birds said, "I turn with soaking shoes, dry leaf and thorn, back to my house...happy to have lived out with you a moment in the wind."

DECEMBER 10, 2006
Evergreens and Mosses

For some, evergreens and other plants are brought into the home during this season, perhaps as compensation for spending less time outside. Fresh greenery may appear in the form of arrangements, potted plants, wreaths or entire trees. Another delightful way to bring the outdoors into our lives is to create a terrarium.

Last weekend my granddaughter and I gathered small samples of peat or Sphagnum, Stair-step and Hairy-cap mosses. Each moss cluster created an intricate ecosystem of ferns, lichens or wood geraniums. We carefully arranged them in a round glass vase, creating a miniature garden. When misted and covered, the terrarium established its own balance. Now it is a joy to peek into the container at a variety of lush green, non-flowering plants and inhale their earthy fragrance.

Mosses provide habitats for a number of small animals, insects and spiders. They also provide fiber for birds' nests and are useful to gardeners in preventing soil erosion while retaining moisture and nutrients. Because they contain a chemical substance that kills germs, peat mosses were historically used by Native Americans for baby diapers and, during World War I, they were used for dressing wounds.

It's time to take a closer look at these wondrous little plants before they are blanketed with snow.

JANUARY 5, 2004
Seeking Color

Now, in the depth of winter, everything seems to be at
a standstill. Even shadows are few and far between. Worse
than black and white is a flat, gray landscape. Yes, the oak
and beech leaves, still clinging, provide some color and a
rustling sound, but they are tattered and lifeless. The days are
getting longer though and, when the sun does break through,
we sense a new quality of light, a new angle of light, and
briefly anticipate spring. The willows already have an amber
glow, verifying that winter will pass, in time.

Just as we have surrendered and burrowed into this
monochromatic month, something extraordinary occurs. The
backyard feeder, resembling a school playground, explodes
with activity and strong, primary colors...red, yellow and
blue. Cardinals, Evening Grosbeaks and Blue Jays cluster and
compete. Their size and movement, their feathers and wings,
create unforgettable moments in time. What a perfect gift!

While January is a wonderful time to burrow, we must be
on the lookout for the surprises that make us smile. They are
everywhere and perhaps more appreciated now than at any
other time of year.

JANUARY 8 , 2005
Gray Squirrels

Working near a window, on a relatively warm day for
January, I was distracted by the sight of a very lively Gray
Squirrel. It looked rather foolish, scurrying up and down
tree trunks, flicking its bushy tail in a deliberate way. Soon
another squirrel appeared. Their activity made me curious
enough to read about squirrels of the northeastern region.
I learned that this is the time of year when males begin to
chase females through the trees in preparation for breeding.
Their young are born in March and, at that time, the females
become fiercely protective, driving the males away.

Evidently, squirrels are among the most successful animals
in this part of the world. Relying upon smell, they survive the
winter by eating nuts and other food that had been stored
in small, previously dug pits. Most often there is a separate
location for each item of food.

So apparent in this season are the homes of squirrels.
Placed at the top of trees, usually amidst oaks and beeches,
are large bundles of leaves that are somehow strong enough
to hold the weight of these lively creatures. Alternatively, tree
dens are sometimes made out of old Flicker homes or rotted
openings where branches have fallen away.

How nice to know that, when the squirrels leave their
protective homes in January and exhibit unusually playful
behavior, it can be assumed that spring is just around the
corner.

JANUARY 9, 2006
A Visiting Opossum

Last night, during a walk in my neighborhood, I saw a shadowy object scurry across the street only a few yards in front of me. Although roughly the size of a large cat or small dog, it appeared to stand much closer to the ground and was more awkward in its movements. Hurrying ahead for a closer look I clearly identified the visitor as an opossum. It's always a surprise to see one, as they simply weren't around during my childhood in Vermont. With hairless tails and ears that sometimes freeze and break off in cold weather, opossums do not seem to be well suited to winter yet, lately, something is urging them to move northward.

Opossums, the only marsupials native to North America, are mammals that give birth to highly undeveloped young. A newborn is about the size of a kidney bean and is safely carried in its mother's pouch for the first two months of life.

Distinguishing characteristics of the opossum are that it has a pointed snout and a tail that is long enough to wrap around a tree branch, allowing the animal to hang. When threatened the opossum remains motionless, appearing to be dead. What an odd little visitor.

JANUARY 12, 2007
The Striped Skunk

January's abnormally warm weather, thus far, has provided an opportunity for new patterns to emerge in nature and conditions that are comfortable enough to get out and observe them. Bird feeders have had less activity. Earthworms have been spotted on dirt roads. Confused bats have come out of hibernation. I have seen two skunks roam in a dazed manner during daylight hours. It's difficult to know whether their unusual behavior is due to illness or an interruption of hibernation and natural biorhythms. One skunk was so disoriented that it brazenly approached a neighborhood home and, undeterred by the large family dog, profusely sprayed everything in its path.

That memorable event drew my attention to skunks. Often active in early or late winter, these beautiful creatures are generally dormant in mid-winter, holed up in underground dens. The dens, found on hillsides or along fencerows, are usually old Woodchuck, Squirrel or Badger homes that have been "renovated" with new grasses and leaves. A foraging skunk will investigate dens that it comes across and may relocate a number of times in one season, often exchanging with Opossums and Raccoons. Up to twelve skunks, mostly female, may live in one burrow.

The Striped Skunk prefers fields and woodlands but can be found in urban areas. It usually forages at night, meandering slowly in search of apples, berries, mice, shrews, nuts, seeds, grains, garbage and carrion. Unlike the other members of the Weasel family, skunks defend themselves with scent rather than speed. However, spraying its scent is a last resort after first trying to lope away, next, turning to face its opponent and stomp its front feet as a warning. Then, it's time to run!

FEBRUARY 4, 2004
Cabin Fever

Black-Capped Chickadees appear jubilant as the winter's deep-freeze begins to thaw. These jaunty little birds, cloaked in formal attire, dine on small seeds, insects and insect eggs found in bark or on twigs. They celebrate the sun by singing and bustling about through gnarly shrubs and lofty treetops... never failing to lift our spirits. At home, we welcome the arrival of these polite and cheerful visitors as they frequent the nearest feeder.

Sometimes, though, my appreciation of the natural world is forced indoors by temperatures too cold to bear. While cooking I may take a moment to savor the deep colors of vegetables, in an otherwise bland season. Leafy green carrot tops are gently removed, leaving the edible roots. Yet, it is the roots that are cut away while salvaging the enlarged stems, and possibly the greens, of crimson red beets. Sliced apples reveal cross-sections of seeds that, as recently as May, were deeply held within gloriously fragrant flowers. The memory of apple blossoms leads me to browse through enticing garden catalogues and to dream of all the possibilities.

In February, I begin to awaken from hibernation, shake off my cabin fever and sleepily peek beyond winter in search of signs that a new growing season is about to begin.

FEBRUARY 12, 2005
Eagles and Ice

There have been a few spectacular days when the sun's warmth has challenged winter's frozen condition. Snow layers seeped into previously plowed fields and dirt roads softened. The expansive lake beckoned skaters with its indescribable beauty. There, in the midst of pale, blue vapor and beneath enormous sky, the mass of solid water yawned and groaned. Sheets of ice had been roughly piled upon the shoreline while the broad surface was finely etched with scribbled patterns of tiny air bubbles.

On one of those days, I walked along a bluff after skating. There, I could hear a crow and soon, the precise, rhythmic sound of a lone skater passing below me. In the distance, rare open water lapped against ice floes. Suddenly, a pair of Bald Eagles appeared a few hundred yards to the north. They had perched in a cluster of trees and were diving for fish. One eventually circled toward me. It flew no more than twenty feet above my head and immediately departed. Clearly visible at that distance, were a powerful yellow beak and rounded white head. Its magnificence was thrilling.

I returned to the same spot at the same time for the next three days but the noble pair had moved on.

FEBRUARY 13, 2006
Mourning Doves

Earlier this month I was surprised by a small flock of Mourning Doves. Perhaps they did not feel the need to head south, given the mild weather we have experienced this winter. Although they have been nesting in the same location for the past several years, I was startled by the sudden whistling sound of their wings as they sought refuge in nearby treetops. Usually doves are not strong enough to scratch through snow and ice for their diet of grass, corn, and weed seed or the berries of Pokeweed.

In the coming weeks, I will begin to watch for the male to bring twigs, weeds, pine needles and grass, one at a time, to the female. He will stand next to her or on her back as he provides building material for a loosely made nest. Occasionally he will peck the female under the chin and give a "Short-coo."

Most of us are familiar with the very distinctive, mournful coo of doves typically heard in warmer months. There are two basic calls, a Short-coo and a Long-coo. The first is three short notes and is used during the months of courtship. The latter consists of five to seven notes, usually made by unmated males to attract a female.

Not always benevolent, a male or female dove may raise one or both wings and may even strike another bird when threatened. This response is referred to as *Wing-Raise*.

By attracting Mourning Doves to your yard with a little cracked corn, you may be treated to the sight of intricate rituals of courtship or exciting displays of aggression.

FEBRUARY 11, 2007
Circle of Life

In January of 2007, I wrote about the unusual spring-like weather we were experiencing and the untimely appearances of skunks. Well, that month concluded with below freezing temperatures that have crept into February. Looking ahead, March usually appears as "the time of water" when ice thaws and snow melts, giving way to wild rivers and, of course, our traditional mud season.

Now, having gone "full circle," it was the thrill of feeling the earth stir again in March that originally prompted me to begin these "reflections." My hope is that, along the way, readers of these musings may have been inspired to go outdoors and take a look, to find comfort in the natural world, to reconnect with a time when humans lived more closely with nature.

In this complex period of rapid change, it is useful to take a deep breath and remember "the grand scheme of things." In a time of social polarization, it helps to be reminded of the great interdependence found among all living things. In contrast to material consumption, it is wise to honor our need for such basic necessities as air and water...to remember that our bodies, like the earth, are largely comprised of both fresh and salt water; that our pulse, like an ocean, rises and falls.

So, now in February, I look down toward my feet at the paths of meadow voles, up at the hovering hawks, into the night sky...and ponder the wonder of it all.